STATUE OF FREEDOM. In top of the Capitol Dome is the bronze figure of the Statue of Freedom designed by the American artist Thomas Crawford. It was placed on the dome during the Civil War in 1863. It measures 19-feet, 6-inches in height and weighs 14,985 pounds. Its cost was $ 23,796. The figure is of a woman in flowing robes with her right hand on a sheathed sword, her left holding a wreath and grasping a shield. Her head is covered with a unique helmet encircled with stars and surmounted by a crest composed of an eagle's head and feathers.

UNITED STATES CAPITOL.

The cornerstone of the Capitol was laid by President George Washington in 1793. It is perhaps appropriate that our young nation declared an amateur designer, Dr. William Thornton, winner among the 17 contestants who submitted plans for the design of a capitol. By 1800, the north wing of the Capitol was completed, at which time Congress moved to Washington from Philadelphia. During the War of 1812, the Capitol was partially destroyed a fire set by the British and had to be rebuilt. By 1863, after several extensions, the addition of the dome higher than the original was completed. Nearly 100 years later the east front was extended, but the original character of the building designed by Thornton has remained.

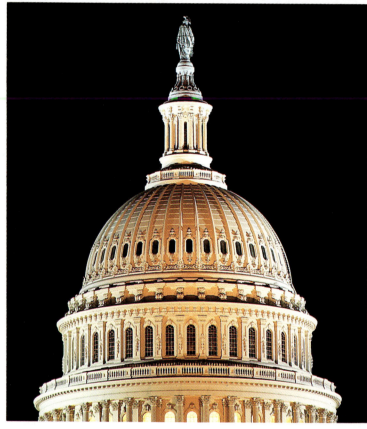

THE CAPITOL abounds in art and decoration, most of which pertains to our nation's history. Most interesting is the Great Rotunda with its 180-foot-high dome and huge fresco by Constantino Brumidi. Statues of Presidents line its curved walls. Other places popular with visitors to the Capitol are the House and Senate Chambers, Statuary Hall and the President's Room. In the Crypt, which features a 12-foot model of the Capitol, structural development of the Capitol can be traced. Surrounding the Capitol is a 68-acre park designed in the late 19th century by Frederick Law Olmsted which includes many noble old trees, fountains and statues.

LIBRARY OF CONGRESS, 1st and E. Capitol Sts., S.E. The massive building was completed in 1897 and shows the influence of the French Renaissance. It is completely decorated with excellent examples of 19th Century art.

SUPREME COURT OF THE U.S., 1 First St., N.E. This home of the highest court in the U.S. occupies a site close to the Library of Congress and faces the U.S. Capitol. The temple like building was designed by Cass Gilbert and completed in 1935. The white marble structure has a monumental entrance with a broad, imposing stairway, a portico surrounded by elaborate Corinthian columns and a sculptured pediment representing "Liberty Enthroned" guarded by "Order" and "Authority".

NATIONAL ARCHIVES BUILDING, Constitution Ave, at 7th St. The final repository for the permanent records of the Government. Outstanding among these are the Declaration of Independence. The Constitution and the Bill of Rights.

FREER GALLERY OF ART, 12th St. and Jefferson Dr., S.W. At the death of Charles L. Freer in 1919, his unusual collection of Far and Near Eastern art was given to the United States, along with a museum to house them. Funds also were given for additional purchases and continued study of Oriental art.

THE SMITHSONIAN ISTITUTION, lovingly called "the nation's attic" was founded in 1846 under the terms of the will of James Smithson, an English scientist who had never crossed the Atlantic. Smithson bequeathed his entire fortune to the United States of America "to found at Washington under the name of the Smithsonian Institution an establishment for the increase and diffusion of knowledge among men". This purpose is carried out chiefly by means of research, exploration, publication, and museum and art gallery exhibits. In the institution's development, ten bureaus have grown up around it, which are now are now considered public necessites and as such are supported wholly, or in part, by Government funds. The institution itself however, is a private foundation, the money having been left in trust to the United States.

top- **THE SMITHHSONIAN MUSEUM CASTLE** in foreground and National Museum of Natural History in background.
bottom- featured here are the Castle, Arts and Industries Building, Hirshorn Museum, and the National Air & Space Museum.

NATIONAL MUSEUM OF NATURAL HISTORY AND MUSEUM OF MAN, 10th St. and Constitution Ave., N.W. Of the 54 million articles in the museum's collection, usually only about one percent is ever on display at one time.

NATIONAL GALLERY OF ART, 6th St. and Constitution Ave., N.W. The marble gallery and many of its great works were a gift made by financier Andrew Mellon in 1937. Over the years more than 200 donors also have given works. It now contains about 2,200 paintings and 1,700 sculptures.

U.S. BOTANIC GARDENS. The Botanic Garden, at the foot of the Capitol, houses a well-maintained permanent collection of both exotic and familiar plants. From September to June, the staff of the Botanic Garden offers a series of horticultural classes on specific plants. A total of 9,000 square feet of exhibition hall features approximately 5,000 species and varieties from around the world, including a Bunya-bunya Tree from Australia. The Botanic Gardens features seasonal flower shows including a summer terrace, a chrysanthemus, and two Chritmas shows. The gardens open daily 9am-5pm; although for June, July, and August the hours are extended to 0am 0pm.
Information 225-7099.

THE HOLOCAUST MUSEUM opened in 1993. 14th and Independence Avenue close to the Bureau of Engraving and Printing.

BUREAU OF ENGRAVING AND PRINTING. The Bureau is responsible for printing any official paper that carriers a monetary value such as postage stamps, money and food stamps. Here you can observe the intricate process involved in producing 7,000 sheets of bills every hour. There are 65 separate steps in the production of paper money including intaglio printing, siderogarphy, plate making, and the actual printing, examining, and overprinting. Security is tight and photography is forbidden. The Bureau began in 1862 with the separation and sealing of $ 1.00 and $ 2.00 bills which had been printed by private bank note companies. Since 1877 all United States Currency has been printed in the Bureau. Tours are conducted from 9:00am-2:00pm Monday through Friday.

JEFFERSON MEMORIAL

A picturesque location on the Tidal Basin compliments the beauty of this tribute to the third President of the United States. The Memorial, designed by John Russel Pope, was dedicated in 1943. The circular, colonnaded monument reflects Jefferson's own taste in architecture, and its domed profile bears a striking resemblance to that of Monticello, Jefferson's home in Virginia. The heroic statue of the President, by Rudulph Rvans, is located in the center of the interior and can be seen through the Memorial's four openings. Quotations from Jefferson's most famous writings are engraved upon the interior walls.

WASHINGTON MONUMENT

Construction of the Monument was begun in 1848 and was completed in 1884, 85 years after the death of Washington in 1799. The white marble shaft rises 555 feet and stands on the Mall, between the Lincoln Memorial and the Capitol. There is an elevator to the observation room which presents the whole panorama of the city of Washington, the Potomac River, and nearby part of Maryland and Virginia. Descending the 898-step iron stairway, one can see the 190 memorial stones presented by nations, states, cities, societies and individuals.

A picture of the **WA-SHINGTON MONU-MENT** featuring cheery blossom near the Tidal Basin.

LINCOLN MEMORIAL

The memorial to our 16th President, Abraham Lincoln is a white marble building of classic design, resembling the Parthenon of Greece. It was designed by Henry Bacon and completed in 1922. The 36 Doric columns of the portico represent the number of states in the Union at the time of Lincoln's death; the walls bear the names of the 48 states in existence in 1922. Inside is Daniel Chester French's famous 19-foot-high marble statue of the seated Lincoln and two Jules Guerin murals, "Emancipation" and "Reunion". Lincoln's second inaugural address is carved in the walls.

THE VIETNAM MEMORIAL is dedicated to the 58,132 men and women who died in service related to the Vietnam War. The Memorial, on the National Mall near the Lincoln Memorial, was dedicated in 1982. It is not the traditional white marble tribute but consists of 2 highly polished granite walls meet to from a "V".

THE NATIONAL ACADEMY OF SCIENCE BUILDING featuring a statue of the world's most famous scientist, Albert Einstein.

THE NATIONAL ZOOLOGICAL PARK, a Federal Bureau under the direction of the Smithsonian Institution, occupies about 170 acres on both banks of Rock Creek near the middle of northwest Washington, D.C. The principal exhibition buildings are the Bird House, Large Mammal House, Small Mammal House, Antelope House, Reptile House, Monkey House and Lion House. In addition, there are many paddocks, cages, and pools dotted about the park along the winding roads and walks between the major buildings. At any one time the Zoo has on exhibition about 3,000 specimens representing about 800 different species; mainly mammals, birds, reptiles, amphibians, with a few fishes, insects and other miscellaneous animal life. The Zoo was established in 1890 for the purpose of preserving some of the animal life in North America that was threatened with extinction. Now, its inhabitants include some of the world's rarest animals.

Washing

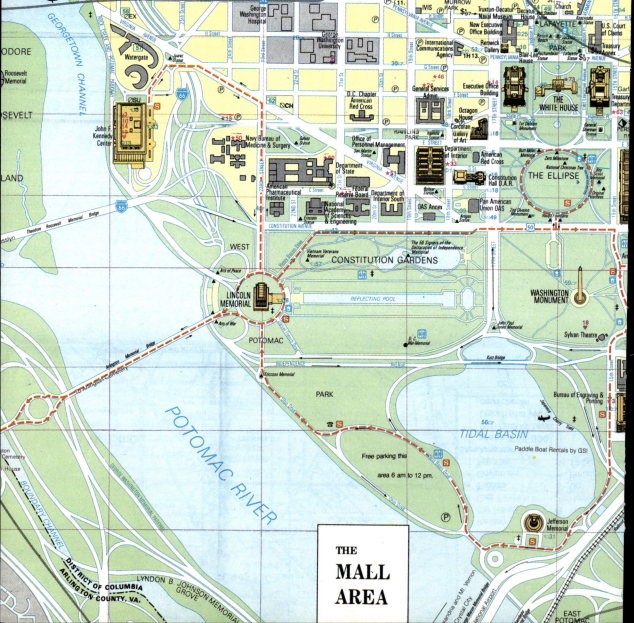

Rentals by GSI ... and National Zoo

GEORGETOWN

ROCK CREEK AND POTOMAC PARKWAY

VIRGINIA AVENUE

ODORE

Roosevelt
Memorial

SEVELT

LAND

GEORGETOWN CHANNEL

Watergate

Juarez
Statue

John F.
Kennedy
Center

☉SU

Theodore Roosevelt Memorial Bridge

sslyn

Arlington Cemetery

Arlington National Cemetery

BOUNDARY CHANNEL

nton
Cemetery
House

DISTRICT OF COLUMBIA
ARLINGTON COUNTY, VA.

GEORGE WASHINGTON MEMORIAL PARKWAY

LYNDON B. JOHNSON MEMORIAL GROVE

POTOMAC RIVER

Foggy Bottom

George
Washington
Hospital

George
Washington
University

H Street

H Street

55 Street

Street

24th Street

23rd Street

22nd Street

21st Street

20th Street

62 ☉CH

★13

Navy Bureau of
Medicine & Surgery

Galvez
Statue

★50

D.C. Chapter
American
Red Cross

Office of
Personnel Management

San Martin
Statue

Department
of State

VIRGINIA AVENUE

★51

★50

American
Pharmaceutical
Institute

23RD STREET

22ND STREET

Einstein
Statue

Federal
Reserve Board

National
Academy
of Sciences
& Engineering

Department of
Interior South

CONSTITUTION AVENUE

C Street

21ST STREET

20th Street

19th Street

WEST

Vietnam Veterans
Memorial
57

Henry Bacon Drive

CONSTITUTION GARDENS

The 56 Signers of the
Declaration of Independence
Memorial

LINCOLN
MEMORIAL

Arts of Peace

Arts of War

18

S

POTOMAC

Arlington Memorial Bridge

Ohio Drive

INDEPENDENCE

AVENUE

Ericsson Memorial

PARK

REFLECTING POOL

D. C.
War Memorial

John Paul
Jones Memorial

Ohio Drive

Free parking this

area 6 am to 12 pm.

P

PENNSYLVANIA AVENUE

IVIS

EDWARD R.
MURROW
PARK

International
Communications
Agency

★46

General Services
Admin.

18th Street

E STREET

Rawlins
Park

Rawlins
Statue

Department
of Interior

★33

19th Street

OAS Annex

17TH STREET

Pan American
Union OAS

U.S. Vet
St
Church

Truxtun-Decatur
Naval Museum

New Executive
Office Building

Renwick
Gallery

52

Blair-Lee
House

Decatur
House

PENNSYLVANIA AVENUE

Executive Office
Building

Octagon
House

State Pl.

Corcoran
Gallery
of Art

American
Red Cross

Constitution
Hall D.A.R.

Boliver
Statue

C Street

25

THE WHITE HOUSE

THE ELLIPSE

Butt-Millet
Memorial

Zero Milestone

National Christmas Tree

Original Patentees

2nd Division
Monument

Haupt Fountains

LAFAYETTE
PARK

Koscuszko
Statue

U.S. Court
of Claims

Treasury
Annex

AVENUE

1st Division
Monument

★63

General
Sherman
Statue

PERS

Garfield
Treasury
Department

50

15TH STREET

WASHINGTON
MONUMENT

Sylvan Theatre

Kutz Bridge

TIDAL BASIN

Paddle Boat Rentals by GSI

Japanese Cherry Trees

Bureau of Engraving &
Printing

56

Jefferson
Memorial

31

EAST
POTOMAC

THE

MALL

AREA

alexandria and Mt. Vernon

Crystal City

National Airport

ton D.C.

WHITE HOUSE
The official residence of the President of the U.S. since it was first occupied by President John Adams in 1800. The Georgian style building was designed by Irish-born architect James Hoban. A prize of $ 500 was awarded to Hoban whose design won in open competition offered by the District Commissioners of Washington. The advertisement for the contest was drawn up by Thomas Jefferson, who also submitted an anonymous plan for the Executive Mansion.

The State Dining Room. The mahogany dining table, surrounded by Queen Anne-style chairs, displays part of Monroe's gilt service purchased from France in 1817. The bronze-dore ornamental pieces are used today as table decorations for state dinners.

The Red Room, one of the four state reception rooms, contains several pieces of furniture from the New York workshop of the French-born cabinetmaker, Charles Honore Lannuier.

The oval Blue Room with many of the furnishings in the French Empire style, the decor chosen for the room by President James Monroe in 1817. Five of the original gilded chairs fashioned for Monroe by Parisian cabinetmaker, Pierre-Antoine Bellange, form the nucleus of the present furnishings.

THE WHITE HOUSE has the simple elegance of a gracious American home. As is the case with many homes of the period, it reflects the design of manor houses in Ireland, England and France. The unique variations which separate Hoban's design are the oval rooms on the south side of the building. Even the casually interested visitor to the White House is impressed by the design of these rooms.

Directly acrooss the street from the White House is Lafayette Square. It features statues and cannon. The buildings surrounding Lafayette Square include Decatur House.

TREASURY DEPARTMENT. The entire Treasury Building covers 5 acres. It is built in a Greek revival style with walls of granite. The existing building is the third one built on the site. The previous two were destroyed by fire. All the area bounding the building is Washington's financial district. There are no public tours of the main building. A reproduction of the Liberty Bell is on permanent display on the west side. A statue of Alexander Hamilton adorns the front of the building.

BLAIR HOUSE, 1651 Pennsylvania Ave., N.W. Built between 1824 and 1827, the house is normally used for entertaining foreign dignitaries. During the reconstruction of the White House, President Truman and his family occupied the Blair House.

THE POST OFFICE PAVILION. This old building at 12th and Pennsylvania Avenue has been converted to a nice collection of shops, including several restaurants. It is built in the Richardsonian Romanesque style of architecture. There is a glass elevator which gives a nice view of the pavilion, in the clock tower. The top of the clock tower is open to the public for a breathtaking view of Washington. Surprisingly this building was scheduled for demolition in 1971, but several groups called for its restoration. It now houses the National Endowment for the Arts and the National Endowment for the Humanities. The tower and shop are open 10:00am - 6:00pm daily. Restaurants are open later for dinner. Information: 523-5691

PETERSEN HOUSE at 516 10th St. N.W. This is the house across the street where Lincoln was taken after he was shot and in which he died the next day.

J. EDGAR HOOVER F.B.I. BUILDING, Pennsylvania Ave., at 19th St., N.W. New home of the Federal Bureau of Investigation.

bottom, Interior of **FORD THEATRE.** The building has been restored to a replica of the theatre as it appeared at the time. It also houses the Lincoln Museum and contains relics, mementos and exhibits highlighting the life and death of the Civil War president.

At 15th Street looking down **PENNSYLVANIA AVENUE** toward the impressive United States Capitol. On Inauguration Day the Presidential Inaugural Parade proceeds down this street.

UNION STATION. Perhaps the most pleasant way to arrive in Washington D.C. is by Amtrak which pulls into this monumental old station. The concourse is the largest room in the world-750 ft long and 130 ft. wide. Union Station is an historical monument renown for the number of soldiers passing through in war. The cornerstone was laid in 1905; it was open in 1907 and completed in 1908. Browse among the three levels and over 100 shops including a food court and movie theater. The station itself is open 24 hours while the shops are open 9am-8pm Monday through Saturday, and 12 noon-6 pm Sunday. There is a five level parking garage in back with two hours free parking (see information desk for ticket). Emerge from the Station, you're greeted by a stunning view of the Plaza and Capitol Building.

WASHINGTON CATHEDRAL, Mount Saint Alban on Wisconsin Ave., between Massachusetts Ave, and Woodley Rd., N.W. Officially the Cathedral Church of St. Peter and St. Paul. It was completed in 1991, and is one of the world's six largest ecclesiastical edifices. Built of Indiana limestone, no steel is used in the construction. Interesting to note are the 300 stained glass windows and seven chapels.

GEORGETOWN began as an Indian trading center. In 1789, the town was incorporated. It boasts some of the most unique boutiques, shops night spots, and a varied range of restaurants.

JOHN F. KENNEDY CENTER FOR THE PERFORMING ARTS, 2700 Virginia Ave., N.W. The founders of Washington envisioned the city as a cultural as well as a political capital for all Americans. That dream became a reality with the construction of a national cultural center that had been conceived and developed under Presidents Eisenhower, Kennedy, Johnson and Nixon. In September, 1971, the John F. Kennedy Center for the Performing Arts opened its doors to the nation. Designed by Edward Durell Stone, the memorial is located on the banks of the Potomac. Its facilities include an opera house, a concert hall and two large theaters, one for drama, the other for films.

Middle left- **WASHINGTON HARBOR** is a collection of fine shops and restaurants in Georgetown.

WATERGATE HOTEL, New Hampshire Ave, and Virginia Ave.

NATIONAL SHRINE OF THE IMMACULATE CONCEPTION: Fourth and Michigan Avenue, N.E. The tribute of American Catholics to Our Blessed Mother as Patroness of the country, the shrine is the largest Catholic church in the United States. The Knights Tower is 329-feet-high; the Dome is 239-feet-high and 109-feet in diameter. The architecture is contemporary, but in the spirit of Romanesque and Byzantine.

PENTAGON BUILDING, Arlington, Virginia. The five-sided giant, nerve center of the Defense Department, is the largest office building in the World. Completed during World War II, it reached a peak strength of nearly 35,000 employees. The interior of the building consists of five floors, two basements, five concentric rings and ten spoke-like corridors. This simple, functional design eliminates considerable walking from office to office.

27

ARLINGTON NATIONAL CEMETERY
Arlington, Virginia

Arlington National Cemetery is located directly a cross the Arlington Memorial Bridge and overlooks the Potomac River and Washington. It was established as a National Cemetery for American military men on June 15, 1864 from 200 acres of the Arlington estate.

ARLINGTON MEMORIAL AMPHITHEATRE. It is used for patriotic assemblies and exercises on occasions such as Memorial Day. A grand colonnade and a large number of boxes surround the outer perimeter of the theatre. It has a seating capacity of about 5,000.

TOMB OF THE UNKNOWN SOLDIER guarded night & day.

ARLINGTON HOUSE, R.E. Lee Mansion. It was here that Lt. Robert E. Lee and Mary Ann Randolph Custis were married in 1831. Thirty years later he was to face an extremely difficult decision, accept General Scott's offer as Commander of the Union Army, or resign his commission and join the Confederacy to fight for his native state.? After the war the Lees never lived here again. To the right of the portico is the tomb of Pierre L'Enfant.

JOHN F. KENNEDY GRAVE. The gravesite of the 35th President of the United States. Here burns the eternal flame which was lighted during the burial service. The view at right was photographed from Arlington House and shows Memorial Bridge with the Lincoln Memorial in the background. (Bottom right).

U.S. MARINE CORPS WAR MEMORIAL. Felix W. De Weldon's masterpiece depicts one of the most dramatic events of World War II, the raising of the Stars and Stripes on Mt. Suribachi, Iwo Jima. Dedicated November 10, 1954, it is the largest sculpture ever cast in bronze.

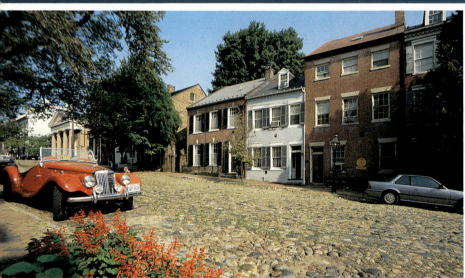

top- **THE WATERFRONT OF OLD TOWN ALEXANDRIA** featuring the Torpedo Art Center.
middle left- CAPTAIN'S ROW in Old Town Alexandria.
bottom right- **LEE-FENDALL HOUSE** in Old Town Alexandria.

Middle right, **GEORGE WASHINGTON MASONIC MEMORIAL.** Built by contributions from Masons throughout the country as a memorial to our first president. It was opened to the public in 1932.

top left- Washington's Grist Mill.

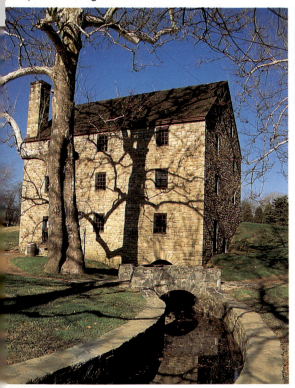

MOUNT VERNON
Mount Vernon, Virginia

Mount Vernon, the home of George Washington, is beautifully situated on the west bank of the Potomac River, 15 miles south of Washington, D.C. Mount Vernon was erected about 1743 by Lawrence Washington, half-brother of the First President. George Washington subsequently inherited the estate with thousands of acres of rolling land. It was the family seat of the Washington family until 1860, when it was purchased by the Mount Vernon Ladies Association, as a national shrine. After Washington's death, in 1799, he was buried in a simple vault southeast of the house. His remains and those of Mrs. Washington were later reinterred in the present tomb, west of the old grave site. The Association's technical staff have recovered many of its original treasures and are exercising great care in its restoration. One of the most effective improvements is the reconstruction of Mount Vernon's formal gardens. A large hothouse provides many of the conventional and exotic flowers and plants popular with the Washington. Other buildings on the grounds include a kitchen, smokehouse, barn, carriage house, servants' quarters, schoolhouse for Mrs. Washington's grandchildren and a Museum.